W9-BIC-885

Around the Alphabet

Connie Major Williams

Around the Alphabet

A new way to look at letters

By Connie Major Williams

Major for Minors
Publishing Company

Copyright © 1999 by Connie Major Williams
All rights reserved.

Library of Congress Catalog Card Number:
98-91347

ISBN 1-892092-00-X

Published in the USA by:
Major for Minors Publishing Company
8134 Huron Street
Dexter MI 48130

To Kevin, Loren,
my mom and sister, and to
Sister Margaret Ann,
who I hope would
have been proud of me.

Aa

Around
Ring around the rosy,
Pocket full of posy,
Ashes! Ashes!
We all fall down!

Bb

Bouncing

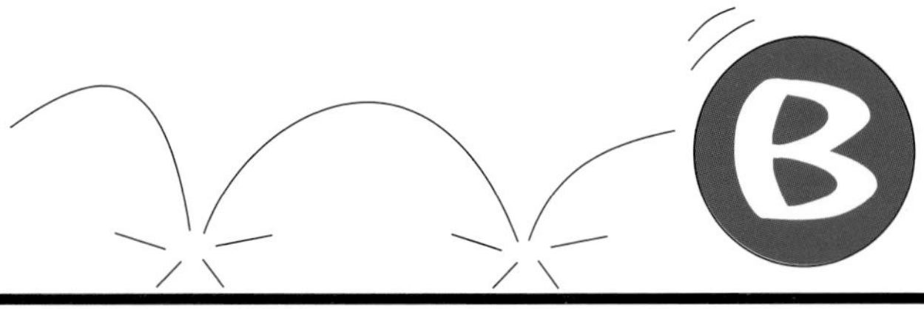

Great A, little a,
Bouncing B
The cat's in the cupboard
And can't see me.

Cc

Coloring

Dd

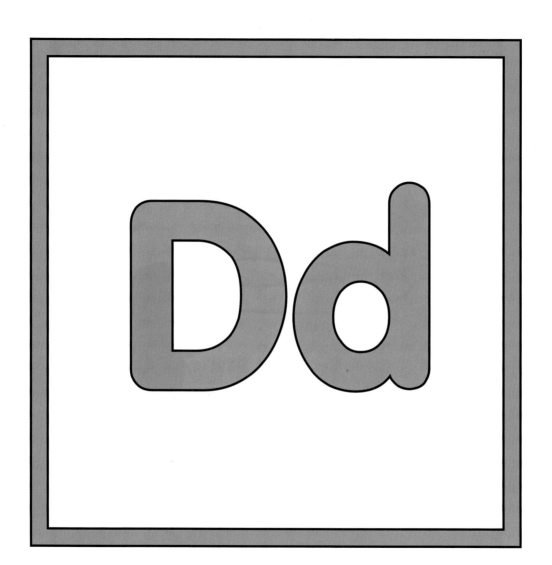

Drippy

Ee

Empty

Ff

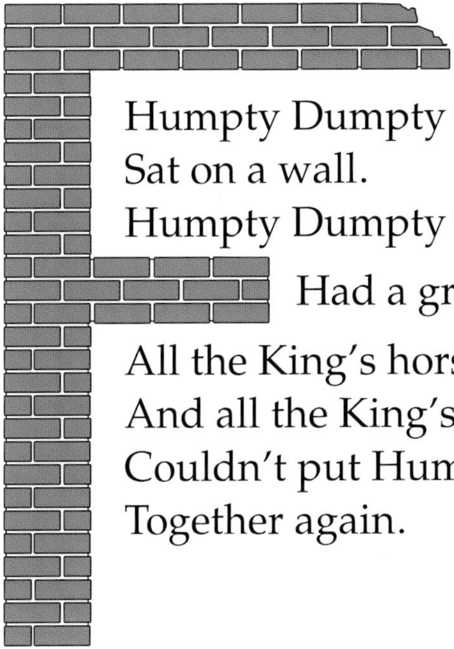

Humpty Dumpty
Sat on a wall.
Humpty Dumpty
Had a great *f*
a
l
l
.
All the King's horses
And all the King's men
Couldn't put Humpty
Together again.

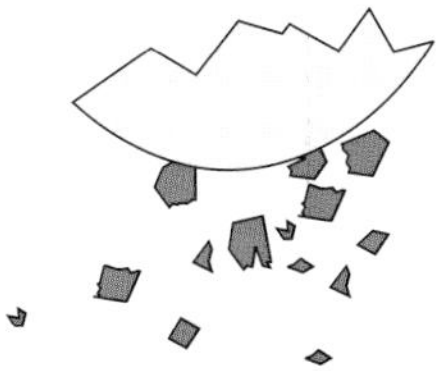

Gg

GROW

Mistress Mary, quite contrary,
How does your garden grow?
With silver bells and cockle shells
And pretty maids all in a row.

Hh

HUGE

Ii

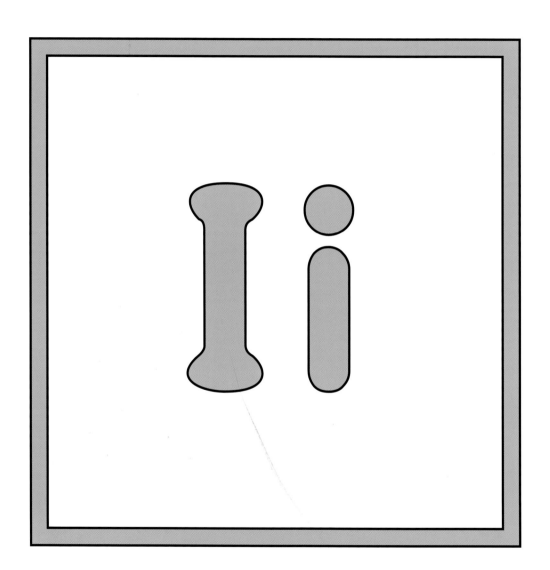

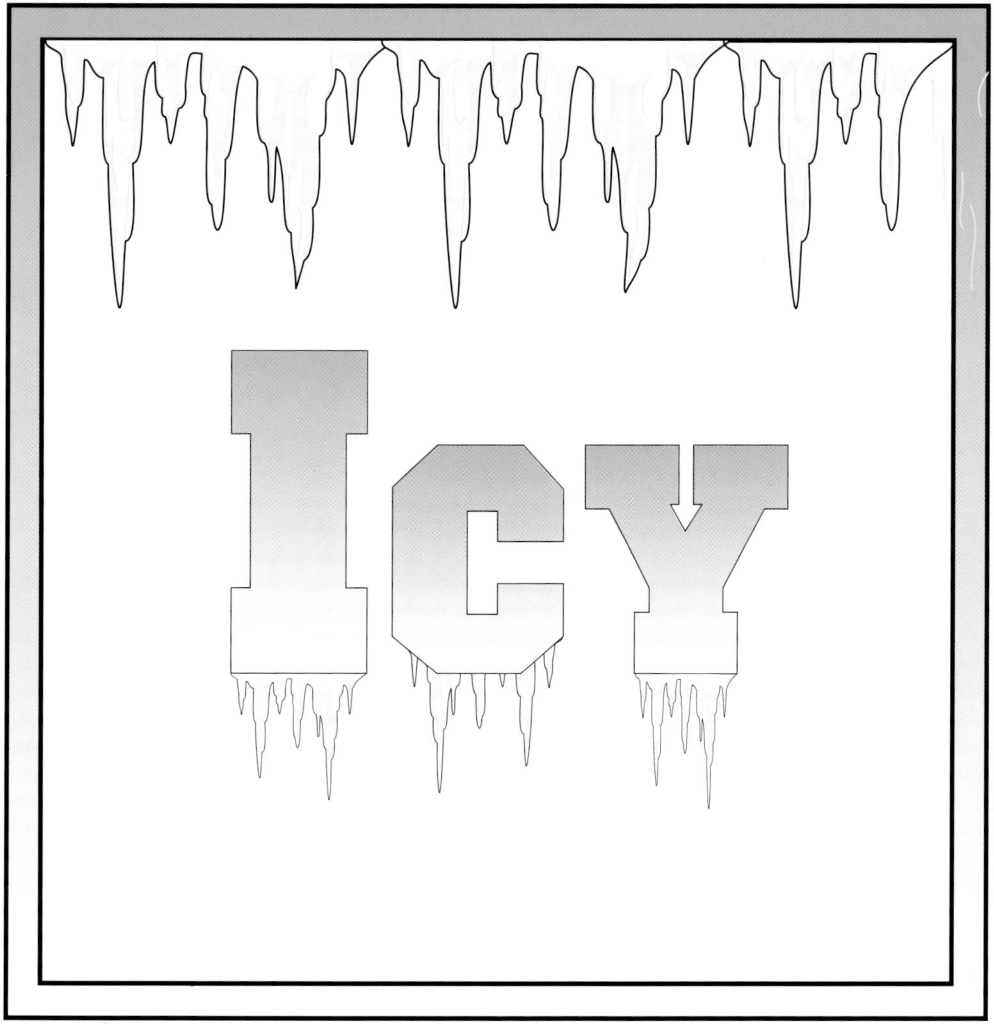
ICY

Jj

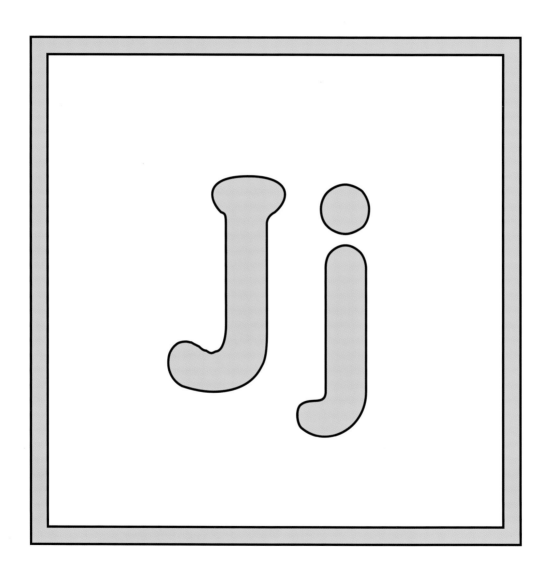

Jack be nimble,
Jack be quick,
Jack jump over
The candlestick.

Kk

Kick

LI

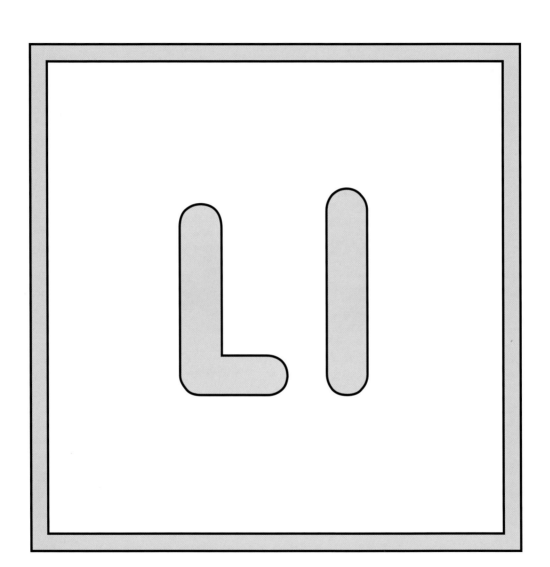

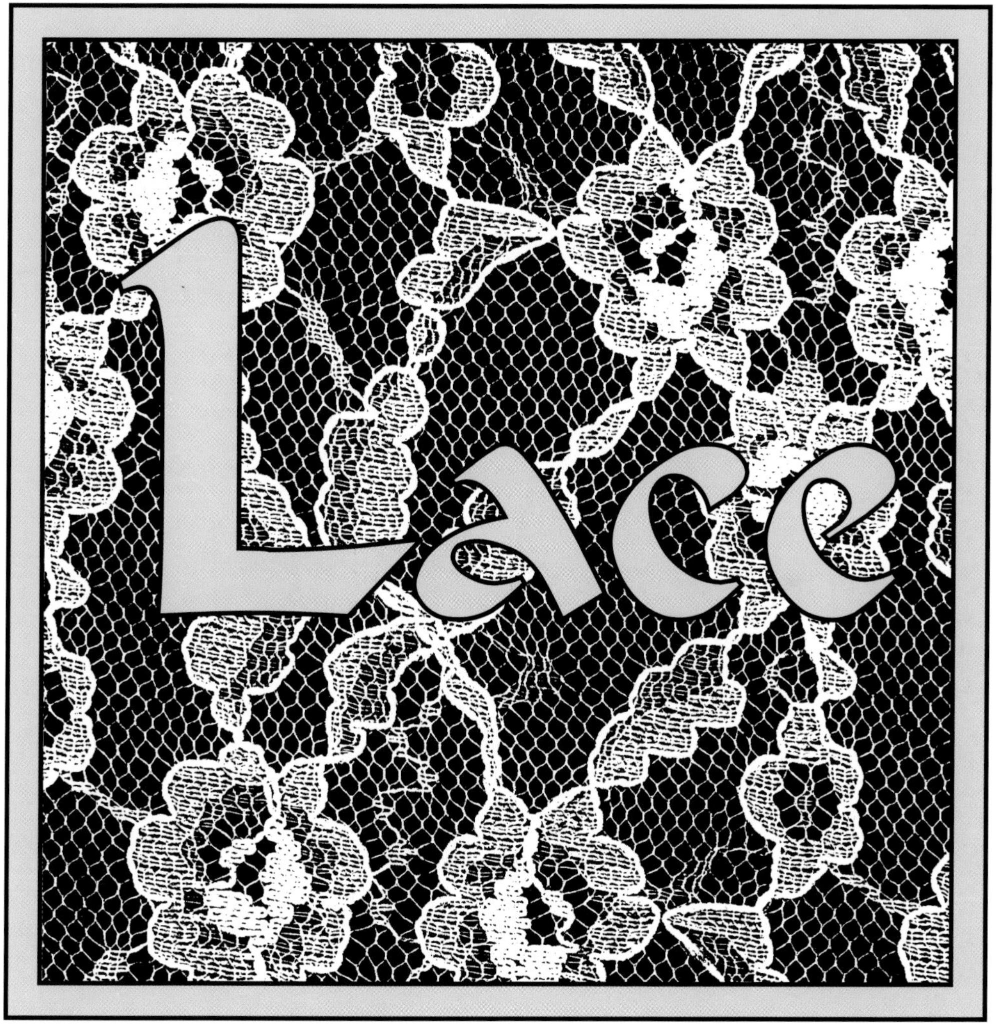
Lace

Mm

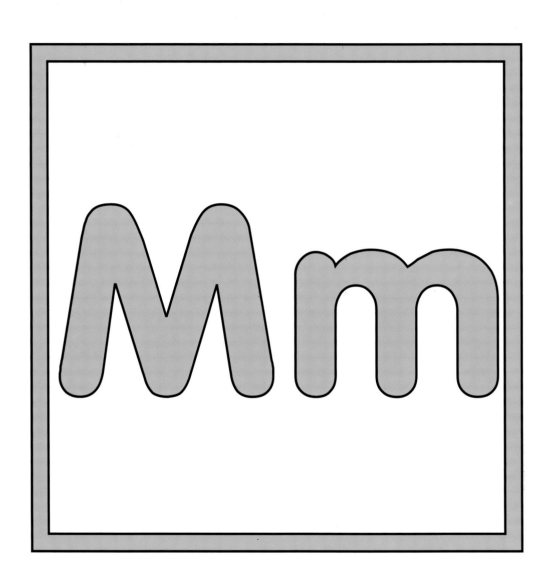

MELTING

Nn

NAIL

Pitty
Patty
Polt!
Shoe the wild colt.
Here a nail,
There a nail,
Pitty Patty Polt!

Oo

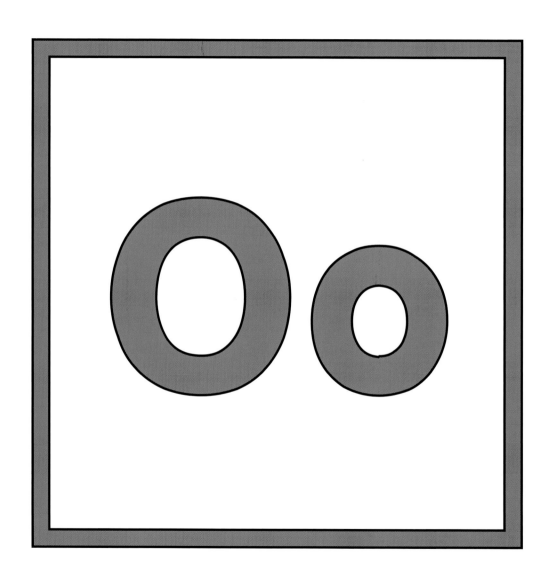

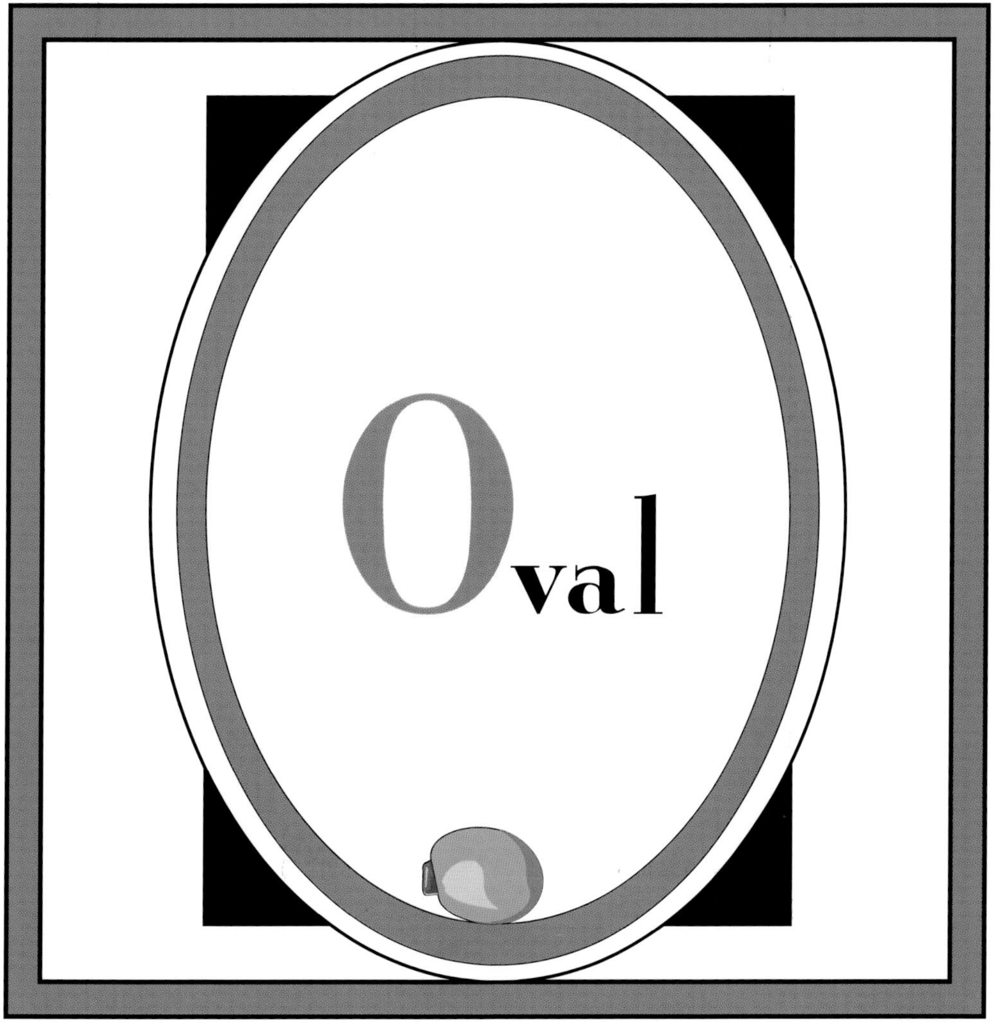
Oval

Pp

Painting

Qq

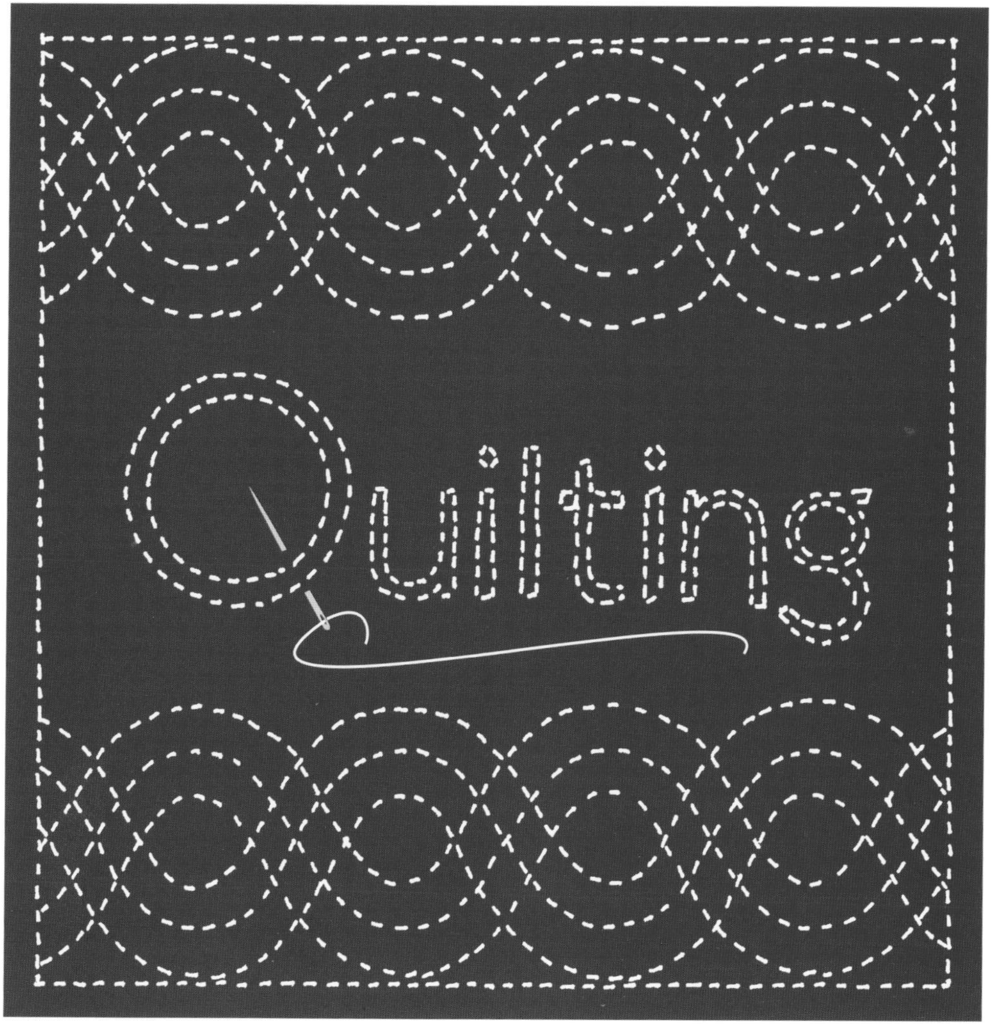
Quilting

Rr

'Round and 'round the rugged rock
The ragged rascal ran.
How many R's are there in that?
Now tell me if you can.

ROUND

Ss

Sloop

Tt

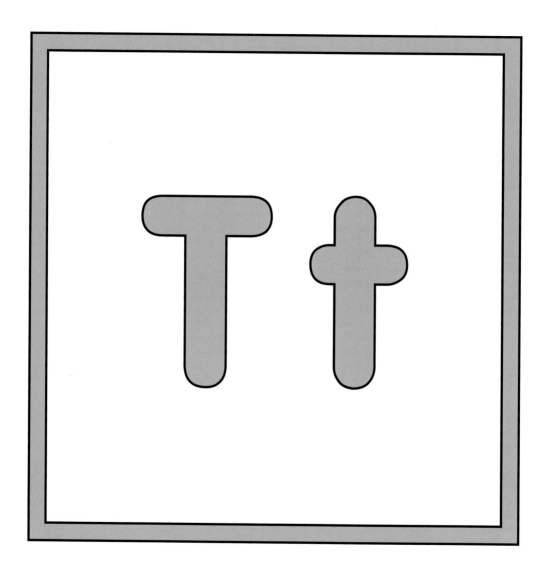

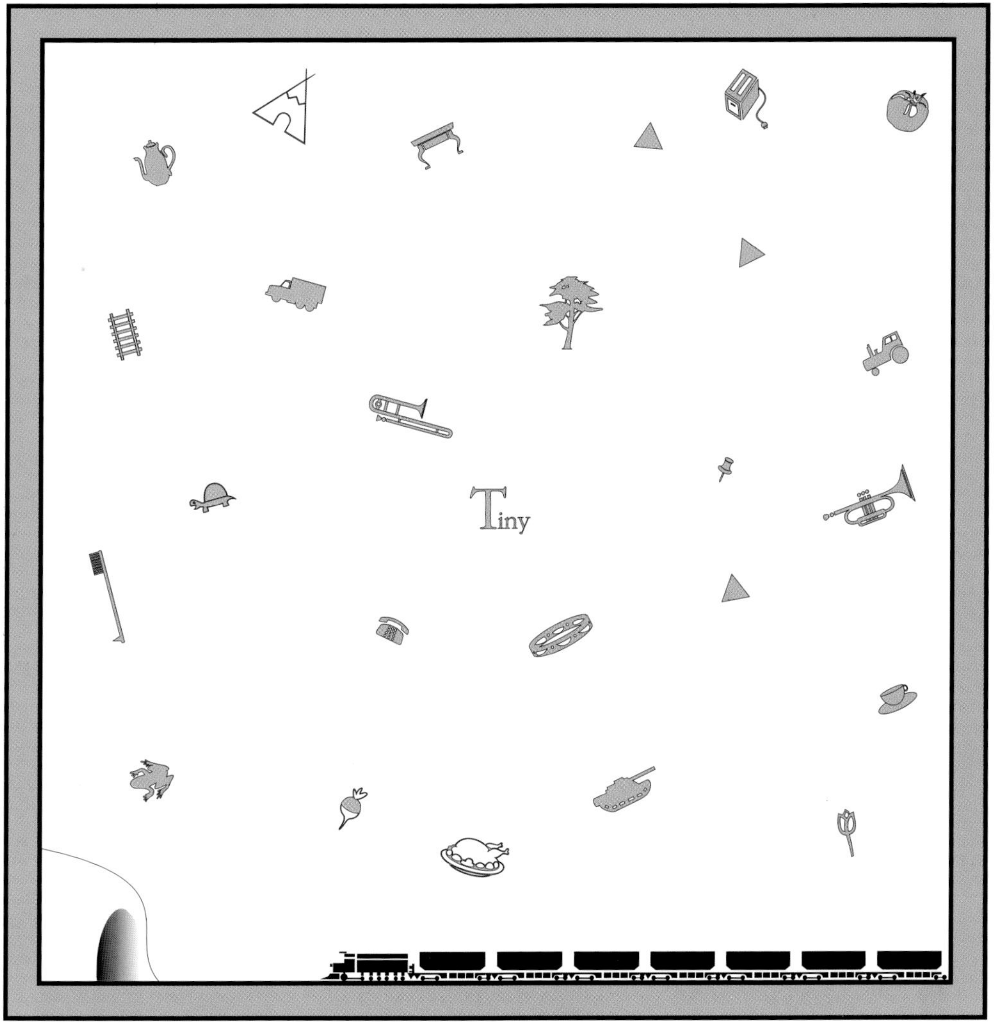
Tiny

Uu

Upside down
Unicorn

Vv

Vanishing

Ww

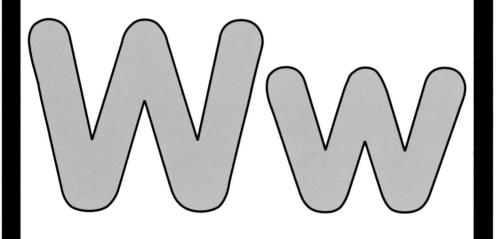

Wiggle

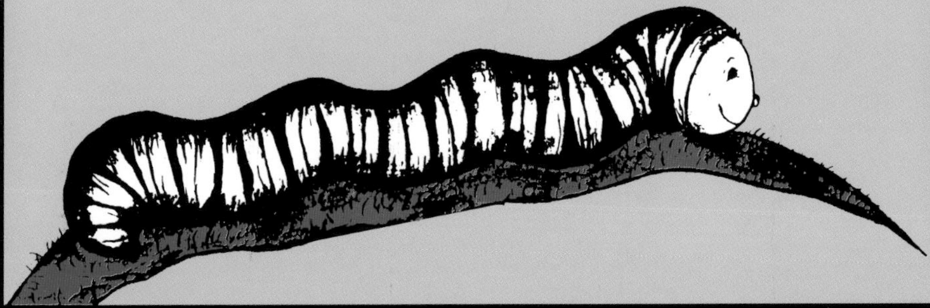

Xx

X-RAY

Yy

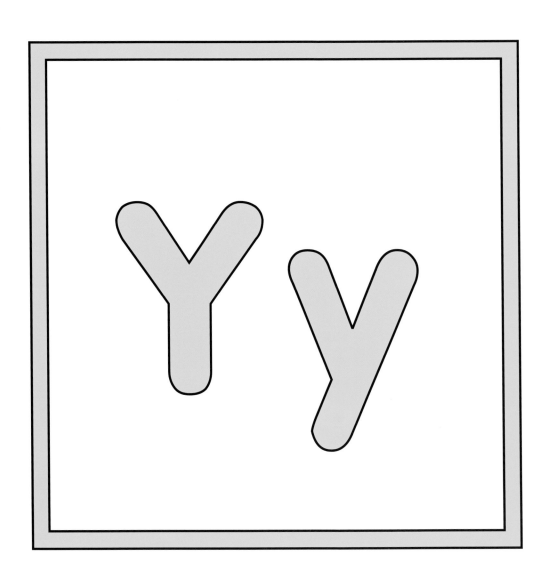

Yellow

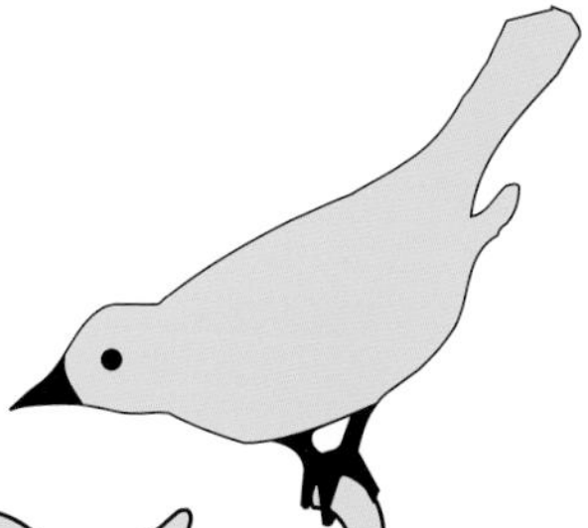

Mary had a pretty bird,
    Feathers bright and yellow,
Slender legs, upon my word,
    He was a pretty fellow.

Zz

Zoom

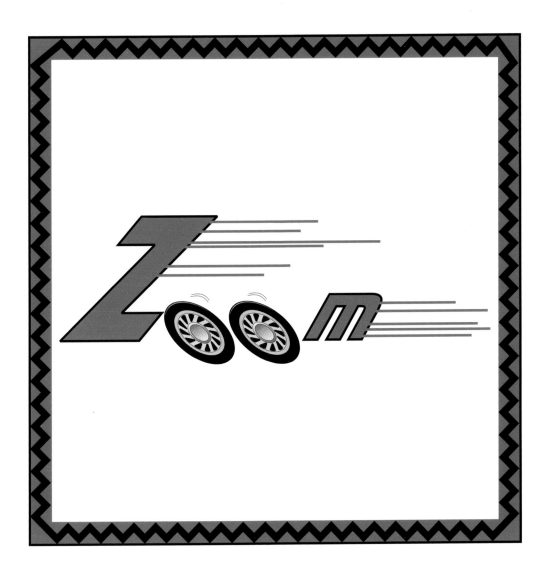

A B C D

E F G H I

J K L M

NOPQ
RSTUV
WXYZ

a b c d

e f g h i

j k l m

n o p q
r s t u v
w x y z

Q C L O R
Z B H M P G
K E V I N
U T X Y S
D F J W A

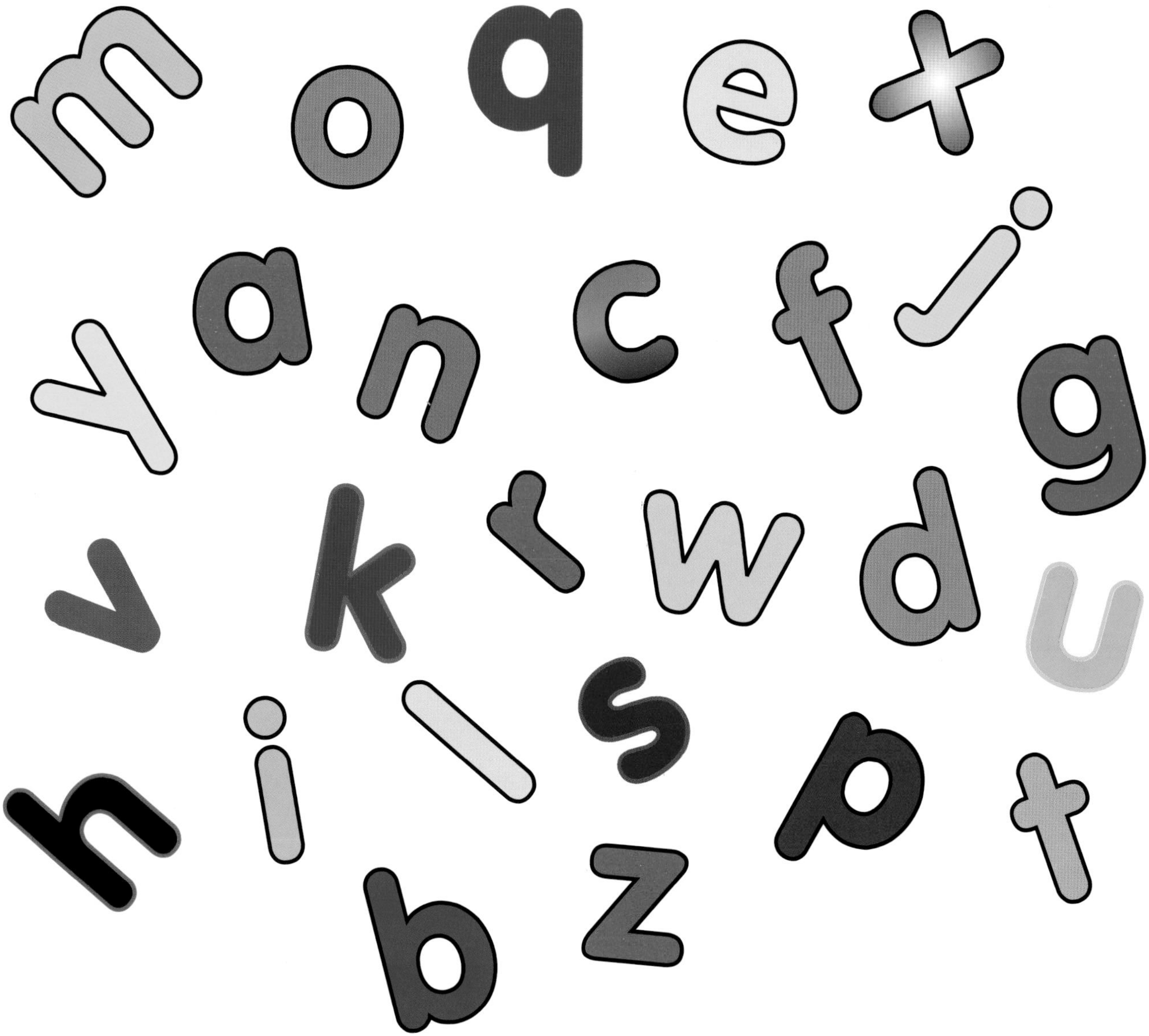
m o q e x
y a n c f j g
v k r w d u
h i l s p t
b z